Oil Spills

by Christine A. Caputo

Consultant:
Ian R. MacDonald
Professor of Oceanography
Florida State University

CAPSTONE PRESS
a capstone imprint

First Facts is published by Capstone Press,
151 Good Counsel Drive, P.O. Box 669, Mankato, Minnesota 56002.
www.capstonepub.com

Books published by Capstone Press are manufactured with paper
containing at least 10 percent post-consumer waste.

Library of Congress Cataloging-in-Publication Data
Caputo, Christine A., 1966–
Oil spills / by Christine A. Caputo.
  p. cm.
Includes bibliographical references and index.
Summary: "Provides information on oil spills, including causes, effects,
and cleanup efforts"—Provided by publisher.
ISBN 978-1-4296-6658-9 (library binding)
ISBN 978-1-4296-6765-4 (paperback)
1. Oil spills—Environmental aspects—Juvenile literature. 2. Oil
spills—Cleanup—Juvenile literature. I. Title.
TD427.P4C365 2011
363.738'2—dc22

2010034343

Created by Q2AMedia
Sr. Art Director: Rahul Dhiman
Art Director: Joita Das
Designer: Manish Kumar
Illustrator: Bibin Jose
Photo Researcher: Akansha Srivastava

Photo Credits
t= top, b=bottom, l=left, r=right, c=center
Cover page: Michel Gunther/Bios/Photolibrary.
Title page: Wimclaes/Dreamstime.
4: Dmitriy Shironosov/Shutterstock; 4-5: Ssuaphotos/Shutterstock; 6–7: Frontpage/Shutterstock; 6: Martin Leigh/Oxford
Scientific (OSF)/Photolibrary; 8: Banol2007/Dreamstime; 9: Danny E Hooks/Shutterstock; 10-11: Wimclaes/Dreamstime;
12-13: Kent Wohl/ US Fish and Wildlife Service; 14-15: U.S. Coast Guard photo; 16: Patrick Nichols/ U.S. Gulf Coast/U.S.
Navy photo; 17: Petty Officer 3rd Class Walter Shinn/ U.S. Coast Guard photo; 18-19: U.S. Coast Guard photo; 20l: Petty
Officer 3rd Class Colin White/U.S. Coast Guard photo; 20r: Petty Officer 3rd Class Nathan W. Bradshaw/U.S. Coast Guard
photo; 21l: Petty Officer 1st Class Krystyna Hannum/U.S. Coast Guard photo; 21r: Petty Officer 3rd Class Robert Brazzell/
U.S. Coast Guard photo
Q2AMedia Art Bank: 12, 15

Printed in the United States of America in North Mankato, Minnesota.
092010   005915R

Table of Contents

Oil and Earth

Where does gasoline come from? What is used to make both electricity and plastics? The answer is oil.

Oil that comes from the earth is known as **petroleum**. It is formed from tiny plants that lived in the oceans millions of years ago. Oil is one of our most valuable **natural resources**.

OIL FACT

The word "petroleum" comes from two Latin words meaning "rock" and "oil."

petroleum—oil from the earth that is used to make fuels

natural resource—a material people use that is found in nature

5

Oil and Water

Pour oil into water, and watch what happens. The oil floats on top! It's easy to see that oil and water don't mix. Oil and water don't mix in nature, either.

An **oil spill** happens when oil accidently gets into the **environment**. Spilled oil spreads across the top of ocean water. It forms a thin layer called an oil slick.

OIL FACT

More than 706 million gallons (2,700 million liters) of oil seep into the oceans every year.

oil spill—an accident that releases oil into the environment

environment—the living and nonliving things in an area

7

Oil and the Environment

Oil in ocean water sticks to living things such as shrimp and crab. Fish that feed on those animals take in the oil. The fish may get sick or die.

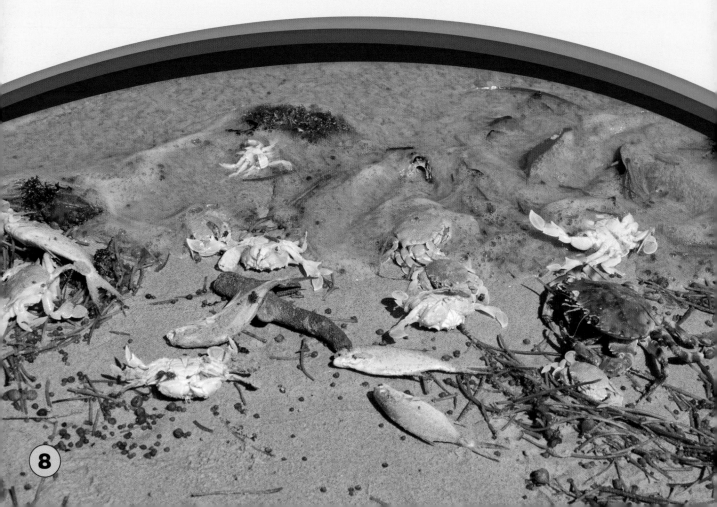

On beaches, oil sticks to sand and rocks. It washes into **wetlands** and sinks into the soil. Plants take in the oil through their roots. The oil damages the plants. It also harms animals that eat the plants.

wetland—an area of land that is covered by water

Oil-Covered Animals

Oil covers animals' fur and feathers. This coating makes it hard for them to swim or fly. The animals may even be poisoned when they try to clean oil off their bodies. Oil can also cover young birds in their nests and kill them.

OIL FACT

Thick oil can also coat birds' eggs. It can stop the eggs from hatching.

Battered Ships

Many spills happen when ships carrying oil are damaged. In 1989 the *Exxon Valdez* hit shallow land underwater.

The ship broke open and spilled oil into Prince William Sound in Alaska. This spill was one of the worst in history. It is affecting plants and animals even today.

ALASKA

Valdez

Day 1
Day 2
Day 3
Day 5
Prince William Sound
Day 4
Cordova
Day 6
Gulf of Alaska
Day 8
Montague Island
Day 7
Day 8

NORTH PACIFIC OCEAN

OIL FACT

The *Exxon Valdez* dumped about 11 million gallons (42 million L) of crude oil into the water. That is enough to fill 20 Olympic-sized swimming pools!

Offshore Oil Rigs

An oil rig is a platform built in the ocean to drill for oil. Oil rig accidents can quickly spill thousands of barrels of oil.

In 2010 an explosion rocked an oil rig known as *Deepwater Horizon*. Oil gushed from a well on the ocean floor for nearly three months. Soon, oil reached shores all along the Gulf of Mexico.

MISSISSIPPI   ALABAMA   GEORGIA

LOUISIANA   Gulfport   Mobile

New Orleans

Tampa
FLORIDA

GULF OF MEXICO

Naples

⭐ Location of *Deepwater Horizon*
◦–◦ Range of oil spill

Cleaning Up the Mess

One way people contain oil spills is with **booms**. A boom is like a fence that is put into the water. Booms stop the oil from spreading. Most booms are filled with air. Others are made from hair, fur, or feathers.

boom

boom—a tubelike structure that floats on water and stops oil from spreading

skimmer

A boom gathers oil into one area. Then boats with machines called skimmers pull oil off the water. A skimmer works like a vacuum cleaner for water.

Efforts Big and Small

People clean up oil that reaches shorelines. These people are called oil spill **responders**. They hose down rocks and sand. They rake soil and clean animals.

Oil spill responders sometimes spray bacteria on the oil to help speed the cleanup. **Bacteria** are tiny living things that break down oil over time.

responder—a person who helps at emergencies
bacteria—one-celled living creatures

Saving Wildlife

Oil spill responders also save animals that are covered in oil.

1 Responders rescue, feed, and warm a bird.

2 They give the oily bird many bubble baths.

3 Warm air dryers help the bird's feathers get back to normal.

4 The clean, healthy bird goes into a safe environment.

Oil spills can affect the environment for years. World leaders are looking for ways to stop oil spills from ever happening.

OIL FACT

It can take up to 300 gallons (1,136 L) of water to clean the oil from just one pelican.

Glossary

bacteria (bak-TIHR-ee-uh)—small living cells

boom (BOOM)—a tubelike structure that floats on water and stops oil from spreading

environment (en-VYE-ruhn-muhnt)—the natural world of the land, water, and air

natural resource (NACH-ur-uhl REE-sorss)—a material found in nature that is useful to people

oil spill (OIL SPILL)—an accident that releases oil into the environment

petroleum (puh-TROH-lee-uhm)—a thick, oily liquid found below the earth's surface

responder (ri-SPON-der)—a person who helps at emergencies; responders clean up oil spills

wetland (WET-land)—an area covered with water for at least part of the year

Read More

Beech, Linda. *Exxon Valdez's Deadly Oil Spill*. Code Red. New York: Bearport Pub, 2007.

Dils, Tracey E. *Oil Spill Cleaner*. Dirty and Dangerous Jobs. New York: Marshall Cavendish Benchmark, 2010.

Faust, Daniel R. *Sinister Sludge: Oil Spills and the Environment*. Jr. Graphic Environmental Dangers. New York: PowerKids Press, 2009.

Internet Sites

FactHound offers a safe, fun way to find Internet sites related to this book. All of the sites on FactHound have been researched by our staff.

Here's all you do:

Visit www.facthound.com

Type in this code: 9781429666589

Super-cool stuff! Check out projects, games and lots more at www.capstonekids.com

Index